NOT FOR THE ACADEMY:
Lesbian Poets

ed. Lilian Mohin

First published by Onlywomen Press, Limited, 1999
Radical Feminist Lesbian Publishers
40 St. Lawrence Terrace, London W10 5ST

ISBN 0-906500-60-5

British Library/Cataloguing-in-Publication Data.
A Catalogue record for this book is available from the British Library.

Cover design © Tyra Till
Cover calligraphy © Kirsten Burke
Cover photo, editor © Katharine Radclyffe

Typeset by Chris Fayers Associates, Lower Soldon, Holsworthy, Devon.
Printed and bound in Great Britain by Mackays of Chatham plc.

CONTENTS

POLEMICS AND POETRY

This anthology is about poetry – not sociology. Of course, it's undeniable that feminist activism over the past thirty years has made nearly everyone aware of the risks and, to a lesser extent, the political implications, of 'going public' about sexuality. In this volume, lesbians show our literary skills.

Long ago, after studying English Literature, joining political movements and "coming out" during England's second wave of feminism, I edited *One Foot On The Mountain*, an anthology of British Feminist Poetry. Contributors to that book had responded to the 'calling' that is poetry and/or to the women's liberation movement, categories that were neither mutually exclusive nor expressed in that order. Published on the crest of the '70s wave of feminism, OFOM is as much a political statement of those times as it is Literature, with a capital I.

Have times changed? Since – say – the 1970s? When in doubt, everyone seems to say so and usually this means something is or, more often, used to be wrong. But for me, and for the work I've collected from poets in *Not For The Academy*, the changed times are right. Years of dedicated, public feminism have, indeed, changed the world.

Now as we approach the year 2000, poets with work in *Not For The Academy* can laugh at, and with, the selves we were back then. For example, "Passing for Not Unusual: Conditions for Graduation at 48" by Elana Dykewomon, says: "all that early women's movement poetry – so much of it was garbage/wave after crashing wave of jane loves jane and daddy did me wrong/still/progressive movements/need poetry". Elana disparages but also praises those efforts because they made a wholly novel impact in literature AND in politics – no mean feat.

And yet, I'm writing this preface in summer 1999 after a series of hate induced bombs in England, the most recent of which was directed at the "gay community" in London. And I'm conscious of the fact that while no good citizen tolerates murder, hurtful discrimination, public or private, is another matter. British and European Union laws provide *no* general protection against discrimination on ground of sexual orientation; and in North America, the legal situation for lesbians and gay men varies according to, at least, geography. So, I tend to see not so much changed as confusing and challenging times.

This anthology of poems by famous (and less well known) lesbian poets is, intentionally, international in scope. It bridges not only the Atlantic, that well known 'pond' between English speaking nations, but also the poetic cultures developed on each side of it. Lesbians under 30 and over 70 years old, of several ethnicities, have contributed passionately skillful verse to NFA.

Here, forms, or dialects, best known in a particular country, don't prevent seeing through to the heart (a word I use advisedly) of their topics. For example, Rosie Bailey picks up, takes off from, and dusts down popular culture as we know it in England; references to advertisements for telephone service in "It's Good To Talk" and brand names for clothing in "Sisters" work even when we don't know the commercial shorthand. Minnie Bruce Pratt sets her loving lament, "The White Star", inside a very American place; yet that scene is known whoever, wherever we are. And while Jackie Kay tries her hand at working-class, Scots dialect in "Maw Broon Sees a Therapist" with lines like: "Crivens! This is jist typical", she leads the reader, anywhere, to agree: "therapy's making me crabbit".

I want to thank Marilyn Hacker for introducing many of the American poets I've selected for NFA. What began as a small(ish) nearly all British anthology, is now held together by an international commonality of attention to metre, syntax, tone and emotional range. And what Wordsworth once called "the grand elementary principle of pleasure" is also here. Enjoy!

Lilian Mohin

ALEIDA RODRÍGUEZ

The First Woman

She was my Sunday school teacher
when I was just seven and eight
He was the newly hired pastor,

an albino, alarming sight
with his transparent eyelashes
and mouse-pink skin that looked like it

might hurt whenever she caressed
his arm. Since Eva was her name,
to my child's mind it made great sense

that she should fall in love with him:
He was Adán. Before the Fall
and afterward, her invert twin.

And she, Eva, was blonde as well,
though more robust, like Liv Ullmann.
I loved her honey hair, her full

lips; her green eyes a nameless sin.
(Not that I worried all that much–
the church was Presbyterian.)

In Sunday school, her way to teach
us kids to pray was to comment
on all the beauty we could touch

or see in our environment.
My hand was always in the air
to volunteer my sentiment.

Since other kids considered prayer
a chore, the floor was usually mine.
My list of joys left out her hair

but blessed the red hibiscus seen
through the windows while others bowed
their heads. Her heart I schemed to win

with purple prose on meringue clouds.
—For who was Adán, anyway,
I thought, but *nada* spelled backward?

While hers, reversed, called out, *Ave!*
Ave! The lyric of a bird
born and airborne on the same day.

But it was night when I saw her
outside the church for the last time;
yellow light, mosquitoes, summer.

I shaped a barking dog, a fine
but disembodied pair of wings
with my hands. She spoke in hushed tones

with my parents. The next day I would find
myself up north, in a strange house,
without my tongue and almost blind,

there was so much to see. This caused
Cuba, my past, to be eclipsed
in time, but Eva stayed, a loss.

Ave, I learned, meant also this:
Farewell! I haven't seen her since.

Concierto de Aranjuez

Vast yellow plain, heat and the meander of memory, incandescent
edge wavering between shadow and light

opens into bright space, the long hot distance vibrating
between us and desire like an empty yellow house

where we'll never live, the unrequited sun reaching for us
so far below, spendthrifts of its attention

even as it flatters us, aimless on this yellow
plain, interminable as a sermon, but–suddenly–olive trees,

grey-green in the distance, hint at moisture,
the mouth of the beloved parting in the shade.

Our pace quickens and a slight swagger loosens our gait,
foreplay originating in embodiment, our own delight

seeking its twin in the beloved,
our mouths small mountain lakes remembering rain,

we are wet with ourselves, and a melodic curve enters
our bloodstream the way the sky releases its blue snake

into water, breaking the hot surface with such deep wetness,
astonishingly blue to the taste,

its edge cold on our parched
tongues, our sweaty necks, our salty faces,

and where time had seemed childhood's summer,
it now rushes with water's

impatience not to preserve narrative but to squander
the moment, an always that seems to bubble from us,

its language loose, emphatic in its surrender,
possession of itself a gift,

now, at the oasis, replacing the plain burning in our eyes
with water, water gazing at sky.

*Notes: Written by Spanish composer Joaquín Rodrigo in 1939, this piece
of music became a jazz standard when Miles Davis and Gil Evans
recorded it on their 1959 album Sketches of Spain. This poem was
inspired by the version recorded by Jim Hall in 1975.*

*Aranjuez was the name of the royal palace in the town of that name
situated on the River Tagus, southeast of Madrid.*

MARILYN HACKER

Scars on Paper

An unwrapped icon, too potent to touch,
she freed my breasts from the camp Empire dress.
Now one of them's the absence of a breast
with a lost object's half-life, with as much
life as an anecdotal photograph:
me, Kim and Iva, all stripped to the waist,
hiking near Russian River on June first
'79. Iva's five-and-a-half.
While she was almost twenty, wearing black
T-shirts in DC, where we almost met.
You lay your palm, my love, on my flat chest.
In lines alive with what is not regret,
she takes her own path past, doesn't turn back.
Persistently, on paper, we exist.

Persistently, on paper, we exist.
You'd touch me if you could, but you're, in fact,
two thousand miles away. And my intact
body is eighteen months paper: the past
a fragile eighteen months' regime of trust
in slash-and-burn, in vitamin pills, backed
by no statistics. Each day I enact
survivor's rituals, blessing the crust
I tear from the warm loaf, blessing the hours
in which I didn't and in which I did
consider my own death. I am not yet
(statistically) a survivor. That
is sixty months. On paper, someone flowers
and flares alive – I knew her. But she's dead.

She flares alive. I knew her. But she's dead.
I flirted with her, might have been her friend,
but transatlantic schedules intervened.
She wrote a book about her Freedom Ride,
the canny elders whom she taught to read

– herself half-British, twenty-six, white-blonde,
with thirty years to live.
                              And I happened
to open up *The Nation* to that bad
news which I otherwise might not have known.
(Not breast cancer: cancer of the brain.)
Words take the absent friend away again.
Alone, I think: she called, alone, upon
her courage, tried in ways she'd not have wished
by pain and fear: her courage, extinguished.

The pain and fear some courage extinguished
at disaster's dénouement come back
daily, banal. Is that blurred brownish-black
mole the next chapter? Was the ache enmeshed
between my chest and armpit when I washed
rogue cells' new claw, or just a muscle-ache?
I'm not yet desperate enough to take
comfort in being predeceased, share anguish
when the Harlem doctor, the Jewish dancer,
die of AIDS, the Boston seminary's
dean "succumbs after brief illness" to cancer.
I like mossed slabs in country cemeteries
with wide-paced dates, candles in jars whose tallow
glows on summer evenings, desk-lamp yellow.

Glowing on summer evenings, a desk-lamp's yellow
moon light peruses notebooks, houseplants, texts,
while an ageing woman thinks of sex
in the present tense. Desire may follow,
urgent or elegant, cut raw or mellow
with wine and black ripe figs: a proof, the next
course; a simple question; the complex
response; a burning sweetness she will swallow.
The opening mind is sexual and ready
for embrace, incarnate in its prime.
Rippling concentrically from summer's gold
disc, desire's iris expands, steady
with blood-beat. Each time implies the next time.
The ageing woman hopes she will grow old.

The ageing woman hopes she will grow old.
A younger woman has a dazzling vision
of bleeding wrists, her own: the clean incisions
suddenly there, two open mouths. They told
their speechless secrets, witnesses not called
to what occurred with as little volition
of hers as these wounds.
                        Passionate precision
of scars, in flesh, in spirit. I'm enrolled
by mine in ranks where now I'm "being brave"
if I take off my shirt in a hot crowd
marching for Women's Healthcare or Dyke Pride.
Her bravery counters the kitchen knives'
insinuation that the scars be made.
With or despite our scars, we stay alive.

"With or despite our scars, we stayed alive
until the Contras or the Government
or rebel troops came, until we were sent
to relocation camps, until the archives
burned, until we dug the ditch, the grave
beside the aspen grove where adolescent
boys used to cut class, until we went
to the precinct, eager to behave
like citizens."
                        I count my hours and days,
finger for luck the word-scarred table which
is not my witness, shares all innocent
objects' silence: a tin plate, a basement
door, a spade, barbed wire, a ring of keys,
an unwrapped icon, too potent to touch.

Broceliande

for Marie-Geneviève Havel

Yes, there is a vault in the ruined castle.
Yes, there is a woman waking beside the
gleaming sword she drew from the stone of childhood:
hers, if she bore it.

She has found her way through the singing forest.
She has gotten lost in the maze of cobbled
streets in ancient towns, where no lovely stranger
spoke the right language.

Sometimes she inhabits the spring cities
architects project out of science fiction
dreams, but she illuminates them with different
voyages, visions:

with tomato plants, with the cat who answers
when he's called, with music-hall lyrics, work-scarred
hands on a steering-wheel, the jeweled secret
name of a lover.

Here, the water plunges beneath the cliff-face.
Here, the locomotive purrs in the station.
Here, beneath viridian skies, a window
glistens at midnight.

Languedocienne

for K.J.

This morning the wind came, shaking the quince tree,
making trouble in the chicken yard.

The attic door blew open, windows slammed their
      casements,
notebooks and envelopes slid off my worktable.

A poplar separating vineyards whispered over
olive and lavender cotton, two shades of summer brown.

Wind makes my head ache. I long for water
surfaces, light on four different riverbanks,

silver trembling on the edge, a waterfall
come up inside me as I come down to you.

Early to the train station; slow bus back through Monday-
      shuttered towns;
nectarines under the poplar, wind in the quince tree.

Marilyn Hacker

Going Back to the River

for K.J.

Dusk, irridescent gasoline floats on the
rain puddles, peacock feathers on macadam.
   Schoolgirl beneath an awning pulls her
   collar up, here comes her bus. She's gone now.

Nine-thirty, and there's light behind thunderheads.
Storm over, in an hour it will rain again.
   Meal done, across the street a neighbor
   shakes out her tablecloth from the window.

I have a reading lamp and an open book.
Last glass of wine, last morsel of Saint-André
   prolong my dinner and my chapter
   into the ten o'clock Haydn program.

What will I say to you when I write to you?
(What would I say to someone who isn't you?)
   I'm home, I've cleaned the kitchen, taken
   charge of my solitude, taken long baths.

What do I tell myself when I open and
write in the notebook keeping me company?
   Don't stay indoors tomorrow morning.
   Do the week's shopping at Sunday market.

Go to the river, take what it offers you.
When you were young, it guarded and promised you
   that you would follow other rivers
   oceans away from a landlocked childhood.

Yes, I indulge myself in hyperbole
since I'm not going out for a walk in this
   wet weather, though I'd walk from someone
   else's place, stop on the bridge, look over.

Seine, Thames and Hudson (sounds like a publisher):
one river flows down into another one.
    Where did I sit and read alone, who
      walked with me which afternoon, which evening?

There was a river when I was leaving you.
That morning, with our *café con leche*, we
    slouched on a bench above the Hudson,
      washed in the wind of a near departure.

Not rupture: each one went where she had to go.
Still, I'd be hours and borders away from you.
    We bluffed like adolescent soldiers
      at the significant bridge or crossroad.

"Your father," you said, "would have been proud of you."
"My mother never would have imagined it."
    Poor Jews in an antagonistic
      city, they pulled in their walls around them.

One city would have looked like another one:
hard work, a clean house, food without seasoning.
    Scrub Europe from a neutral palate,
      blend and assimilate, mistrust strangers,

know in an instant which are the *lanzmänner*.
No Yiddish pet names, gossip or baby talk.
    Brownshirts outside the door would pass on
      innocent, bland Mid-Atlantic Standard.

Is any accent that safely nondescript?
Their child, I bruise my brain on two languages
    (neither the one they lost) four decades
      after they earned me this freedom, passing

as what they weren't: rooted American.
Their daughter, I come home to two continents,
    live with my roots tied up in parcels,
      still impecunious, maybe foolish.

Another child of children of immigrants
(Russian, Italian), you've chosen languages
    written in symbols meant to have no
    country of origin, color, gender

(though every symbol's chiseled with history).
There, you are learning chemical formulae:
    meals on the run, a book you started
    months ago under the bed, abandoned.

Life's not forever, love is precarious.
Wherever I live, let me come home to you
    as you are, I as I am, where you
    meet me and walk with me to the river.

JUDITH BARRINGTON

The Dyke With No Name Thinks About Landscape

1

At first it wasn't landscape at all.
Where you live is just where you live:

a place to walk about in,
drive your car through on the way to somewhere,

notice on a pretty day
when clouds are puffs and grasses blowing just so.

From a horse's back, tracking the skyline
grey sea became grey sky

and chalky paths down the escarpment
gashed the smooth flank of the downs.

Leaning over to unhook the chain
of a five-bar gate, she knew

just how fast to sidle the horse through
before the metal gate swung back with a clang

and the horse twitched an ear—
too familiar with the sound to make a fuss.

The windmills, Jack and Jill, spread their sails
and grew as organic as gorse bushes

or hares on the barren plough
but their spread sails remained unmoved

by the great wind which stirred up a great wave
in the grasses from Firle to Beachy Head.

Up there on her horse she too grew
organic as winter wheat

never naming the villages far below:
Poynings, Ditchling, Fulking, Steyning

distant clusters of roofs that revealed to her,
as if through a telescope,

a particular lytch-gage, a brick well,
a pub she knew: *The Wheatsheaf.*

2

When she left it became landscape–
a beloved green painting hauled around in her mind

while the next one (ochre and sage) unfolded
smelling of Mediterranean pine in the afternoon

and the one after that (sepia and umber)
threw open its chest and sang.

In these landscapes too, she wanted to grow organic–
spreading her limbs to the sky

on that almost-flat rock that jutted from the river
and held her between two swirling streams.

Pinpoints of spray pricked her skin
which dried and dried between the divided waters

while the river too–turbulence, rocks,
moss, trout, and human body–

pried open the hot thighs of the desert
with the persuasive pressure of wetness.

Was it then that it started–
then she began to feel the eyes watching?

In each landscape, people grew from the shadows.
In each landscape, people belonged.

But here on her rock,
head in the V of the parted waters

the dyke with no name sees herself
as if with eyes watching from the hill above,

sees the desert intersected by river,
sees ponderous rocks, shaggy falls, the cruising hawk,

and herself, a human figure growing from shadows,
herself in the frame, on the rock, not belonging.

3

The trouble is not nature, she thinks,
but the people who tell you there's always one of each—

starting with Noah
and his couple-filled floating zoo.

Pistils and stamens, winged seeds from trees,
insects waving their various appendages:

she remembers her smudgy drawings from biology;
she knows what they left out and why.

The trouble with pastoral scenes is the lovers—
the hand-in-hand, one-of-each, "lover and his lass."

She knows it's more than looking wrong in the picture.
But does she know it's a matter of life and death?

4

Whose life? Whose death?
All she wanted was to move again like the winter wheat

to live in her skin touching the earth's skin
to feel spray and rock and the finger of the sun.

Once, long time ago, she made love
on a hilltop under copper beech trees:

leaves turned to mulch underneath her
as she breathed the sky through her lover's hair

and somewhere close by a pony snickered—
a friendly snicker; an acknowledgement.

She still remembers what it felt like to lie in those arms:
some of them beech roots, others human and female,

trusting the pony like a brother,
the sky looking down the same way she looked up.

That was before the two hikers were shot—
the two women, stalked for days by the man.

who killed one and left the other for dead.
One each for life and death as it turned out.

5

There is nothing organic about cars.
They skim across surfaces, separated

from the landscape by hard, black tarmac:
no danger of putting down roots.

Even when a car disintegrates in the ground,
blackberries filling the bent frame of its windshield,

rusty chassis sinking into the earth
to blue up some passing hydrangea,

even then, its chrome and oil and plastic seats
spurn the comfort of ordinary rot.

The dyke with no name kept moving,
her rubber tires grabbing the blacktop with a squeal

as she pushed sideways through bends,
kept everything skidding.

Tall haystacks with poles poking out the top
dashed by her window. She noted their shape,

their resemblance to some señorita's hair
held up by a protruding pin.

She watched the show through glass
as if she put in her penny on the pier,

watched herself from the hillside above
speeding through picture after picture

silk headscarf flying, arm on the door tanned
hands turning the small leather wheel.

Sometimes, when her head raged with pain
she parked the car in a field and slept,

all doors locked, all windows up
while the grasses tickled the hot skin of her tires.

6

Now she is lying on a blanket, the sand below
moulded to the shape of her body.

Sudden swells slap the shore beyond her feet:
a barge has passed by,

trudging down river with its load
like a good-natured shire horse
its throbbing lost now behind the breaking
of that great wave which seems to rise from the deeps.

The turbulence is quick: a lashing of the sand
followed by September's lazy calm

as the river moves unseen again,
cows from another world low on the far shore

and the seagull's body, a fragile handful,
dangles gently between its two tremendous wings.

The trouble is not nature, she thinks
but the people who say I'm not part of it.

They're trying to paint me out of the landscape
says the dyke with no name

but her thighs in hot sand remember a horse's warm back
as the wind makes a great wave from Oregon to Beachy Head.

Why Young Girls Like To Ride Bareback

You grasp a clump of mane in your left hand,
spring up and fall across her back;
then, pulling on the wiry black hair
which cuts into your palm and fourth finger,
haul yourself up till your right leg
swings across the plump cheek of her hindquarters.

Now you hold her, warm and alive, between your thighs.
In summer, wearing shorts, you feel the dander
of her coat, glossy and dusty at the same time,
greasing up the insides of your calves,
and as she walks, each of your knees in turn
feels the muscle bulge out behind her shoulder.

Trotting's a matter of balance. You bounce around
unable to enter her motion as you will when the trot
breaks and she finally waltzes from two to three time.
Nothing to be done at the trot but grab again that mane
that feels, though you don't yet know it, like pubic hair,
and straddle her jolting spine with your seat bones

knowing that when the canter comes, you will suddenly
merge–you and that great, that powerful friend:
she, bunching up behind, rocking across the fulcrum,
exploding forward on to the leading leg, and you
digging your seat down into the sway of her back,
your whole body singing: *we are one, we are one, we are one.*

Four Reasons For Destroying A Spider's Web (A Meditation During The Gulf War)

One: It is in your way,
strung across a doorway
or between the forest walls
flanking your trail.
It floats like a mantra
across the steps down from your deck
and you cannot duck under
or walk around the other way.
You've tried.
There is no secret password
at which, when you utter it,
one filament will let go
and the whole web swing back intact
closing silently behind you.

Two: You don't like spiders.
It's not a violent dislike–
just the kind that makes you shudder
when you feel the web caress your face.
Where is the spider? you wonder
as your smallest hairs prick up
and somewhere in your brain
a picture of that arachnoid body
dropping inside your shirt
opens like the iris of the camera's eye–
gone before the thought.
You try to be careful
as you break the web at one corner
and its tenant falls away, glaring.

Three: Spiders belong in the wild
and yours is human territory–
sterile, cleansed of everything that grows
outside your control.
You scrub lichen and moss from bathroom tiles,
smother the prolific earth with concrete,
and watch out for those beasts

that swim and swim through the plumbing.
Somewhere in your immaculate brain
you know a spider's web is a symbol—
not the great grandmother spread across the sky
but wayward nature getting the better of you.
You keep a special broom for the ones slung,
gaudy with dew, between your sculptured shrubs.

Four: Killing things gives you a fix,
so you tear out the web
with one wild grab of your hand
and watch the small body plop down.
When it scuttles away, one step,
one foot grinding it to a pulp
and you smile. Something in your brain
gives a little, eases up.
Sometimes you speak to the body
flattened to a smear on the floor:
"Little bastard," you sneer
and the thing in your brain hums a sweet song.
Or "goddam black fucker,"
as you grind your teeth and grin.

Judith Barrington

Horses And The Human Soul

> Undercover investigators in Tallahassee, Florida
> watched two men break a thoroughbred's right rear
> leg with a crowbar at 10:10 p.m. The men were part
> of a nationwide ring that injured horses to collect on
> insurance policies–*The Oregonian*

1

The bay mare lifts her head and listens.
There is darkness, the new moon barely revealing
trunks of scrub oak beside her meadow.

A car door has slammed.
The mare shifts her hoofs in the wet grass,
her belly round with the sweet spring growth.

Frogs are merely a backdrop of sound–
as much part of her world
as the post and rail fence against which

she scratches her rump
or the *stamp stamp* of Bess and William in the afternoon
when the sun is up and the flies biting.

A figure steps from the oaks, metal scoop in his hand.
He holds it out, jiggles it
til the mare hearts the familiar sound of sifting oats.

2

They say when you dream a horse
that horse is your spirit.

Once the horse I dreamed
looked out of a trailer pulled by an old Volvo,

the driver a woman who one day
would teach me something about the spirit.
She drove carefully.
The horse was safe.

When you dream a horse it had better be safe
or we are all in trouble.

3

Did the investigators hide behind those same scrub oaks?
Did they wear grey suits and carry notebooks as they
pushed their way through the lush undergrowth? Did
their ballpoint pens carry the name of their company?
Did they smoke as they waited for the sound of the car or
did they talk about money or football or the girls in the
office? Did it occur to them then, as the man led the mare
back to his friend with the crowbar, that they could stop
this before it happened? Did the new moon shed enough
light for them to see as the crowbar hit the right rear leg
just below the hock, the blood spurted, the rich brown
hair mixed with splintered bone, and the mare screamed,
or did they have to note which leg it was later, after the
arrest? And what happened to their souls? What
happened to them? I want to *know* that.

4

The brown mare dreams of Bess and William.
In her dream they stand nose to withers
nibbling the itchy spots on each other's necks
swishing tails across hindquarters.

Later, all three of them gallop, heads up
and she feels the wind on her chest
and the sky all around her ears
and the scent of hay in her nostrils.

She bucks as she did when she was a yearling
and when she bucks, her right rear leg
reaches up as if to kick a hole in the sky.
Then, in her dream, a man leaps into a trailer.
She has never thought of kicking a hole in a trailer
or in a man—and she does neither in this dream.
She knows nothing of the state of human souls.
In her dream the man drives carefully and she is safe.

Body Language

The thing that makes me crazy is
how much I wanted her—
the simple act of longing
year after year, till finally
she took my hand and held it
pressed to her small right breast.
That kind of longing
turns your whole torso into a cavern
where despair echoes wall to wall
and hope leaps like a foetus.
My complicity confuses the issue.
How to say the word: *abuse*
when my body tells another story—
not a tale of clenched self-protection
but an epic, my young arm
reaching out for her breast,
my back spreading wide to her touch?

The thing I go back to is
the rain on the window—
water washing all over the pane
as hand moves to breast
and someone seduces someone else.
My complicity clouds the definitions
like that misted window,
one side of its thin old glass
steaming with the heat of breath and skin
while the other
leans into the storm, weeping.

PAT WINSLOW

Cutty

The florin and the sixpence in the purse
is her mother's trust in her.
She will hop skip and jump down the road
look left look right look left again
and cross and cross the great big ocean
the wide Sargasso of cars and buses
all on her own to the Express Dairy
which is blue and white as the foaming sea.

Yo ho ho for a packet of tea
and a bag of sugar
some milk and some butter
to melt by the fire
when the sad coal scuttles
and shunts like worn out
tired old siding engines.

See how the apricot sun is descending
how the cutty surf threads
between green gold and red
and she doesn't stop she runs instead
to the razorbill sharp bird-flapping edge.

She has ruby earrings and a black tarred pigtail.
The snakes on her arms which the first mate drew
with some ink and a nail whilst the crew wasn't looking
she swapped for a kiss when the lookout slept.
Her cutlass is lean as a scolding tongue.
Her limbs are as strong as any boy's.
She climbs up the rigging and scratches the sky
with her sailor's grin and her chart-maker's eye.

See how the petrels are towing her out
past pebbled seals and switch-backed dolphins.
The cormorants dry their boomerang wings

and plunder the peaks for silvery fish.
Her lungs are rasped by the captain's smoke box.
Oh how the petrels are towing her out.

Lagoon! Lagoon!
The last gold doubloons of inlet sound.
She climbs down aft and rows her shallop out.
She shanties the buck and ridge and swell
and drags her boat to the scrunty rocks.
She ties it up with a mooring hitch
and watches the skin of the ripening sun.
Her galleon rides the crease and furrow
safe as a baby, safe as a baby.
It's rocked from its belly
by the anchor below.
The wood the masts the ropes turn black.
She watches she waits and now at last
the sun begins to swallow the sea
drinking it from the tilting cup
on the other side of the world.

Too soon! Too soon!
The first mate rings the angelus bell.
Her kissing mate rings the ship's church bell
St. Edward's Catholic Confessor bell.
He calls her back to the dry bone land
and dusty dusty evensong.

Heave-ho to the red bus Finchley Road
Hoop Lane and all the traffic lights
to the semi-detached October evening
with her mother's order under her arm.
She's walking home to the fire and the sink
to the liver brown lino and the things that click
like dentures knitting and electric lights.
There is twopence ha'penny in the purse.
Her mother's trust in her.

Under the pillow where her dreams spill out
is a bloody nail and a bottle of ink.

She is planning things, great future things
in the blotting paper silence.
Nobody sees the dragon rise
my sister's earth-spinning dragon rise.
Nobody sees its east-west eyes.
Nobody looks that far.

Biscarosse Plage

Hurled you to your knees,
no hand in your back,
no fist to flatten you,
just a rush or a push,
fierce, like being born.
Down, down,
your face among the flinty sand.

You go back in to stand
waist deep, waiting for the lunge,
the long white curl or snarling lip,
terrible ice racing across your breasts.
You jump, turn. Again.
Hurled to your knees.

Later, your heart, tidy and put away.
Sandwiches. A bottle of Badoit.
A landrover stops nearby.
The sea rolls back.
You see her then,
see them lift her in.
Her hair is a vicious slap
across her face.
Her legs are any-old-how.
The red flags flutter.
A beach ball bounces.
Someone calls out *beignets*.
They drive away,
leave tread marks
near the Scandinavian family
with perfect skin.

You stay away after that.
Even the dunes worry you.
Swallowers and spitters out.
Shapes of sea made solid,
collapsible.
You dig a hole and sit in it.
You stay there
till the sun goes down.
Waiting for the green flash.
Waiting for the terror
to be excised from your skin.

Remote Control

Don't go near him, she said.
My father, the myth-man
with the afternoon behind his head,
the white sunshine
reticuled in nylon curtains,
trapped like breath,
like summer air.

The spider-climbing day
spun itself around us.
We were held fast in its spittled silk,
hiding behind doors,
hiding behind walls.
His whiskey-glower
had the look of a twister about it,
the sort of colour you get
when leaves turn inside out
and the sky broils up for something big.

Don't, she said.
The ceiling got lower.
The smoke from his Camels
yellowed everything.
The TV brayed.

I was not afraid, only curious.
He was two-skinned.
He could turn himself inside out.
One night he would show me strides of lightning,
teach me where to look,
how to guess the next attack.
Another, he would make me sit
with one arm tied
until I used my fork.
He was a military man.
He could mark each glass
of Jameson precisely.
His eye was a spirit level.
Horizontal is best.

That's the way he was that day,
when my mother wouldn't go near him,
when no one could,
just the TV,
and even that was in its place.

Steph

First, there was that standing stone of her back,
the flat wedge of her resolve. Her legs grew
later. Her hands, when she held the book,

were neat, exact. She flipped the leather tab,
laid bare the pages in her clefted lap.
Tight, in her filofax, those spare black ribs

of my name, my number, and every
workshop. We scheduled more. Three long wish-bones.
Tuesday, Wednesday and all day Saturday.

Then came signs. A slow ooze and cold trickle
through grass. The sense that somehow a river
was beginning - mossy rocks and pebbles

knocking and shifting, cracking skins for luck.
I shuffled the cards, stared at wax faces,
divined tidal bores and eagres. I struck

iron on stone, heard it ring. Cross, if you dare,
this Rubicon. Hoist the dark coracle
onto your shoulders. Stride bog, fen and carr.

Brave the icy mists. Go on, go on. Out
and to the skire morning with you,
the skirping stones, the river at full pelt.

I went. I did not look back. I took her
with me in a purple rucksack, in pens,
in pockets, on scraps of folded paper.

I played her on my head-set day and night.
I went miles with her. And then it happened.
One warm weekend, as the afternoon light

was sucking diamonds up from the lake,
when I was watching turtles, she caught me,
and I turned around and I caught her back.

In a smile. Just like that. Everywhere
was dazzled out except for one brief thing -
the searing blue of a small kingfisher.

Grass and sun and sky held breath as the world
capsized, rolled Inuit-style and came up
laughing. I never dared believe it could.

Each moment stays intact. Like grains of sand.
I sift them out and watch them mix again.
Her smile, her legs, her back, her open hands.

Massachusetts

Sometimes I feel this country racing in my blood.
On warm damp nights the smell of skunk
is almost cunt, the earth breathes fox and musk.
Bats caper and unseen eyes taunt and thrill,
green and amber in the imagination -
my striding captured in the pupil's dilation,
my white face snapped on a reptilian lens.
Crack. A black thorn tears and snags.
Ferns drip wet, spill rain into my open flesh.
Moths surprise a torchlight frenzy through my veins.
I search my skin for ticks, but not for shame.
I am in love with this muscular land,
this sinuous undergrowth
that tugs my hands and snicks my hair.
Rough: *stay where you are, don't move.*
Soft, beguiling: *dip silver fingers in the moon,*
ripple its face, spool it up like satin.
It's there, it's there, but you can never have it.

By day, the steep rocks dare to break the water
and hurl it to the clefts below.
Canyons, gorged with summer, sweat.
The fattened year ticks on.
Mica winks on the flattened bends of carved out roads.
Cardinal-flowers rise from spiking grass.
Fierce, but never cruel, this biting
and twisting into ground, this drawing blood
down from the sky at dawn, at dusk.
A beaver cleaves the creek and slips its tail
like a slim tongue between two lips of current.
The shadows lengthen, a green so blue and black
you never want to lose it.
Laughing: *come lick the juice from my teeth-*
maple, birch, sumac, oak. Swim, plunge,
sway in my slow, easy Chicopee, straddle my sap.
Measure your flesh against the cool
of my grey moose evening,
rest your heart against me, match my pulse.

Sometimes, I can feel all this
just watching from a lonely Greyhound bus.

MINNIE BRUCE PRATT

The White Star

Inside the White Star it was warm, tumbled clothes
and humming revolution of unsteady, washer-dryers.
It was a whirligig blur of red black blue yellow
that Beatrice watched like a TV, next to her lover.

Last night she'd looked into lighted windows
bitterly, as if she'd been evicted, things thrown
out on the sidewalk, cracked lamp, books sprawled
by the mattress, sheaves of paper spilled, all
looking small and naked, exposed, like her once
in a bad dream of childhood.

                                    Not yet, except
they'd been kicking some people out on her street,
not her, not yet, not for skin or rent money,
but always perhaps if she forgot to draw her curtains
when she kissed the woman who was not her sister,
when they slowdanced in the kitchen before supper.

Not yet, but already to her. The children taken,
no place of hers, lit or dark, fit for home.

Not yet here to her, but already to a white woman
on the block, standing out by her clothes piled out
to draggle-tail in the dirt, in the getting-dark time,
clouds neon pink, birds going to roost so fast
they leave only a single wingbeat in the air overhead.

Already to a brown woman under a mound of blankets
piled by the corner, her head emerging at footsteps,
cautious, fearful, wrinkled turtle neck.
                                    Already
to the sallow woman on a laundry bench, wine skin
hot as a blanket, asleep in the clean drunk room.

Minnie Bruce Pratt

Tonight in the White Star muzak was playing old
brittle raindrops. Beatrice leaned sideways against
her lover, smelling her hair and the clean clothes.

Next bench, a man muttered stones, a woman stared away.

> The padlocked doors, people bending in the rain
> to salvage one obscure object, people shouting
> to no one: *We live here. You can't throw us out.*

She closed her eyes and wished they could dance
in this lit public place. Mouth against the other's ear,
she began to hum: *Go in and out the window, go in
and out.* How the glass would crack under a desperate fist.
Go in and out the window as we have done before—

CAROLINE GRIFFIN

**'Speak what we feel
Not what we ought to say'** - *King Lear*

Could just our hands be lovers?
It would be blameless, easy.
I see yours, deft and muscular,
sewing, writing, playing the piano.
Sometimes you touch my fingers lightly-
the significance I don't pin down

Sunday, Greenwich, grey and cold-
it's an escape. As we talk
wind blasts the rigging of
a tea-clipper which roared
all the way to China.
There's rain on your glasses.

Earlier, I'd touched the muddy river
hoping for salt, hoping to be splashed,
hoping to follow that river's rush
right down to the sea.

I needed drenching, I see now,
as though some words like
'dearest dear'
or 'darling'
(hardly formed) had yet begun
and needed washing off,
needed joining to some formless deep
in which I feel
but no breath has committed me-
inchoate words committed only to the sea.

It seemed
a word once spoken
could not be denied.
I stood on the steps near Greenwich Pier

exuberant, wanting only the slap of a wave,
not realising why that discipline
is kind - it knocks the words away
before they crack my head - 'my
dearest love'.

We walk on, drink some wine.
In a Sunday Restaurant
the people come and go
lapping against this island
where we meet, until one moment
our hands are wings,
beating and recoiling.
You are trying to give me something -
your ring, I say, I'll look after this
for you, and the fluttering settles.
Small waves slide over pebbles.
The disturbance ebbs.

If just our hands were lovers
it would be reaching through prison bars
asserting all that's mortal can be loved -
or branches leaning without blame
or fracture, even wings beat the air
with no remorse.

But we don't live like that -
river-banks pour with smoke,
those burning boats, the ghats of Benares.
Still I hold my hands out to the fire
and see they're scarred.
I hope for something -
though the world spins when I realise it.

Give me gentleness, not just of memory,
to be held as I go on with it - not just
this river, this afternoon, these nights.

'How would you know me in the dark without my voice, my face?'

Because I felt your heart rise up
above my chest, as a bird would sing
after you wrenched the cage's door,
wrenched and tugged yourself against me
and we didn't even care for intricacy
or delicacy   no you would be free
the lunges say (the skier and
the surf-board rider know) and
no time now
no more fluttering against
the door of your coming.

I would know you in the dark because
I felt your heart rise up
as a bird would sing   a
thrilling in your chest
astonishing mine
and how you gradually settled
in the nest of our bones   in
the pool of our sweat   cooling
to an   ah-calm   as your
speckled body came to rest.

So I play the piano and you
stand-lean against my back.
I feel one column forming -
your pubic bone   my spine
and I'm steadying this - Bach -
until wide wing-beats take off
take over and I'm breathing   deep
salt air. It's the bird's eye view
of the great ocean
opening beneath -
moving   saying
something like   compassion.

So it's all one now
and I can remember this surprise -
what we make and
what comes to us
the strong winds   the ocean
and you still standing   and
I am playing the piano.

'Not in entire forgetfulness
And not in utter nakedness
But trailing clouds of glory do we come.'

But it's too early and I'm
turning over   chased by
heat - a hard cat's tongue
insistent and unbearable.

I move to disperse this.
Blind askew I wearily raise it.
Dawn flares behind the High Street
the mass of the terrace - while below
the gardens in their stunned silence
cup the dark.
Dawn is on edge
but nothing there is jarred
yet or spills over.

There is the day
all brimming and slithering.
I will not haul it in
and turn away
trailing my glory like chains.
I am on fire with something
and want to put it out.

My hands are as dry as leaves
as tinder.
I pass the morning through my fingers
and let it fall
praying the watery day
will put me out
before this friction burns
a hole so big I fall through
into nothing.

We used to speculate how
something marked us out for each other -
and certainly there are marks
indelible   irreparable   a sort of
pressing in time.
I don't see you now and no
maybe we don't want to get over it.

Was it some marking we recognised
and were prepared
to breathe it out - lovers' sighs
turning   into flames?
We leaped up from the bed
touched the charcoal-incense
clasped each other round waist and
thigh the break into fire
and whispered contracts
'til oily smoke took hold
and forced us back to watch.

The contracts I forget except it
was hope and wondering now
how I could even strike a match.

I keep thinking
how I try you when I see you -
how I set off
knowing you're holding me
while I'm bolting at this awareness
and blinkered too.

It is a trial. I say -
hold this
I'm a burning piece of coal
and then ice - well that's fear -
and finally a stick
beating the empty air of
why why why do I keep
running away -
as though I can't see you
out of the corner of my eye.

When it began to rain
my loping just fizzled out - I'm
neither coal nor ice nor even
the horse which is bought with sugar
and can't be kissed - I saw
my feet on the damp pavement
coming back to myself
accepting - after this performance
your warm and waiting hands.

Dorset 1996

but think of Pegwell Bay - Victorian
stiff and grey with waves demure
that fold and then retire. And us
on holiday, gentlewomen
intent upon pursuits, improvement,
painting the headland (water-colours),
reading out of doors, poetry.

You shut your eyes to all that
and took off your rings.
I tried them on.
You were playing Queen again.

I knew the signs.
Grey stones burst into flames
where you trod - but I felt tired,
needed improvement, not pursuit.
I told myself - she wears an anorak
                    drinks strong tea
                    tells lies
thinks she's the bee's knees.
Anyway I've given up on stealing.

So, there was idle talk of sex
and planned promiscuity
(the women in their forties).
We looked up from balancing books,
the books of the heart, the chronicles
of all we'd wanted, all we'd lost,
practising that slick talk,
yet secretly trying to care for love,
to feed the heart on more than scraps.

The last night we ate in the garden -
lit a fire against the edging cold
that sloped in and pushed us closer.
I read a poem I'd prepared earlier -
an old memory of passion spent

and finding time's up on that currency.
It was all about hope and I suspect
an attempt to catch something,
someone.

When the fire was almost out
you rose up, lurched into the dark,
returned with ripped hedges,
dripping leaves - luxuriant gesture -
drunk I suppose and grandiose -
the flung branches sizzling dense smoke
until the snapping sparks flew up and up.
My careful friend worried for the thatch,
standing guard as we indulged
in fire and wanton sparks.

Wanton sparks...
I thought you told the truth
when you hoped by the fire's end,
as I leaned forward to catch your thoughts -
tremulous intimacy - when you hoped
to be, in age, attractive to younger women.
I sympathised -
found out later you'd had your fears assuaged
on a cliff top only two days before.
One of your longer walks - and she
the young unknown who went home early.
But not so young. Maybe she had you too,
Siren in walking boots,
who stole a march on us, made
something more to balance.

Dorset-waves that fold and then retire.
Gentlewomen on holiday -
the steadfast watcher of the fire,
the one who loved in her pain,
and me, trying on your rings,
trying to balance the books of the heart.

Caroline Griffin

In the Gallery

1. She finds the comet (*Pegwell Bay*)
   but the bleached faces of the shell-gatherers
   demand more notice. Behind their backs
   the unexpected flared, changing everything.
   Yet caught in this flash of revelation
   they are stoic, disturbed. Some
   return to their labours, in this case
   hands searching cool sand.

2. *The Ghost of Flea* marks
   the radiance of those
   whose gaze matches its own -
   ghost for ghost flickering fire
   which once (corporeal)
   would neatly snap a shell.

3. The smell of snow. Paris
   the unusual light.
   Do you remember?

4. She would walk away
   from her body if she could,
   but the painter (a woman)
   detains her, half-naked
   hands heavy and red with cold.

5. There is more: Alberto Giacometti
   all night my body was troubled -
   transient flesh,
   running like wax
   in the pits of the death camps,
   the rivers of torture.
   You catch us, naked,
   at the point of farewell,
   when all gestures are signals -
   the hand unfurled
   directing our notice,
   but nothing more urgent

than these lips, these sensuous lips
which tell us we blaze
before the dark.

6. After this, found metal,
    detritus of the farm-yard
    welded upright. Even here
    plaintive undulations
    recall the human form
    stranded without tenderness.
    No mouth. No careful rendition
    of thorax or thigh.
    Two standing figures.

7. Two women still standing.

MARIA JASTRZEBSKA

I Am Carrying Happiness

I am happy
it's so simple

I am carrying happiness
in my hands
I scarcely dare breathe
I'm afraid
of dropping it
as though I had to cross a desert
carrying a bowl of water
as though I'd picked up
a baby for the first time

I'm afraid
if I hold it too tight
it might break
and if I hold it too loosely
it could slip through my fingers

suffering wasn't like this
it was much more familiar
I knew where I stood with it
now my feet barely touch
the ground

now I don't know
how to behave at all
I am carrying happiness
in my hands

"He seems to me to be like a god…" Sappho

No God

No god
the man with blue eyes
looking pleased with himself
laughing as he sat next to her.
But he seemed to me
to have everything then.

She begged me
begged me not to say anything.
She said she was sure
he'd never marry her
if he knew.
I let her gag my mouth
with the silkiness of her imploring looks.

So he grinned at me
- the loyal friend -
puzzled that I stayed aloof
he pinched and slapped her thighs
telling jokes,
while I sat in silence
opposite him, tongue-tied
till everything swam before my eyes.

My words
a swarm of bees
hurled their small bodies
against the silence.
Their angry hum
spread like a fever
through my limbs.

Once when I raised my voice
she looked at me with such sorrow
I backed down,
lived for years stinging only myself,

Maria Jastrzebska

hated him
because I didn't know
how to hate her.

Mother and Child I

Crimson and white/fire and ice
alternating like an electric storm

When I was born I almost died
I chanced with death when I was born

Waking in the small hours
before dawn

my mother overheard
the nurses talking

A few hours old
and something cut out

Already caught
by the massive pull of opposites

A nurse christened me
with tap water just in case

My mother watched frantic
as blood battled oxygen inside my skull

Crimson and white/yes no
everything stopped

A terryfying lull
took the place of her joy

Could this be of significance now?
I remember nothing

She watched
as darkness flooded my brain

But I lived
to drink in everything about her

Maria Jastrzebska

Mother and Child II

They tried to fight fire
with ice, packing it around her

sending more shocks
into her already startled body

good girl/bad girl
stop and go.

But nothing
could put her fears to sleep,

no amount of drink
or drugs,

they only made her fear
more unintelligible

like an animal stunned
running in circles.

Her tears ceased to flow
on the outside

seeping instead
into her milk, her blood,

they threaten to drown her.
To this day

she keeps
a constant vigil.

We were never told
what happened to her

only that she'd gone away
for a while.

MAUREEN SEATON

When I Was Straight

When I was straight I dreamed of nipples,
my dreams were crowded with cleavage and yin,
I read a book that said if you are fickle

about sex, note your obsession in dreams
then do the opposite in real life. This
made sense, my boyfriend said, although it seemed

oddly like a game of Exquisite Corpse
to me. We'd make love, I'd dream of figs,
that drizzled pink, and sometimes I'd lapse

into madrigals (meaning: of the womb), big
leap from the straightforward sessions in bed
of linearity and menthol. Legs

would cross and uncross in my dreams, heads
fall back with me at the throat, I adored
the winged clavicle, that link between breast-

bone and scapula. Straight as gin, I poured
myself into pretense and fellatio,
you could count on me for bold orgasms, for

trapeze art and graceful aerobics, oh
there is no lover like a panicked lover.
Once I dreamed of abandoning the Old

Boyfriend Theory of Headache and Blunder-
buss. Believe me, I said, this will hurt him
more than me, but the dream laughed! Torture

me, I thought, now that even my id
has turned against me, there is something fragile
here to lose, exquisite truth, and I did.

JANE MILLER

The Flying Fish and Lily of May

In an hour as yet unspent,
whose very name "forget-me-not"
suggests a golden age of ordinary
people out to see the cherry
flowers gather in the brightness of the flames,

the day
grows dark reminding every guest
a guild of poets who are dressed
in February as plum blossoms
and in August as the tremulous

camellia accompanies romance
and makes of circumstance a rendezvous; in such hour
as deltaic rivers slice the city written
with fine beams of light, and steamy images
rise under bridges down straits

to the sea, I shall be dreaming all the while awake
to hear asked, "How did we bear the pain?," and the world
answer, "Everyone was in it, too,"
such that it will have been miraculous
to have lived our love and sing of it to you.

J.P. HOLLERITH

Chelsea Creek

Through the blank evening of the river bank
No one existing (save emblematic office women
One to a window), we passed flats homely as a hotel,
To the place where the still-living creek joins the river,
And watched the light on the angular faces
Of the smallness of everything. A helicopter provided
One parabola of noise in the muted evening.
I said I'd never fly in one of those; when they fail,
It's the worst death of all, falling and terrified.
You said most people die terrified. I pushed that back to you.
But I do die terrified, every day, imagining
Trying to get used to, without you, some life
That wasn't falling forward into nothingness.
Sitting on a bench with no thought, no sound,
The light falling from the windows to the ground.

April III

Down under the earth something is stirring
Forcing up clods of thick soil rich as fruitcake.
It is a young tree, a shoot, a sapling
Green as thin skin, pliant as grass;
And you ask me why I bother
To come back to you, live in your house.
Habit, just habit. Like Spring
Which returns about this time every year
Without good reason, I am the flock of birds,
The ripening twig. I know nothing more
Than the ebb and flow of seasons.
If I flood you now
It's only because I can't do otherwise;
I am not choosing you.

Word-for-word Translation from an Inflected Dead Language
(For Sappho)

The moon rose above the day-bleached hills.

Who never answered me despite
My supplications?
I understood…

       …chariots in the summer's dust
The avenue of laurels along the flat land.

My heart flamed like a coal suffused
With air from the open door
Opened by a glimpse of you.
Are there gods of love?
…
Looking at a blue harbour
Thinking of you in sandals and
Someone else's arms.

J.P. Hollerith

Iphigenia

Bound and tasting the stone's dust
Iphigenia could see clearly, upside down
Her father's knees and the edge of his war tunic,
The greaves of his troops, circled round,
Their spear butts in the earth, and far off
At the corner of her eye, a wink of sea.
She knew by the tightening of her father's hand
That he was about to embark on her throat-cutting
Took a last breath of his sweat and the oily knife.
Then the reversed world disappeared in a folding cloud.
She saw the slender trunks of birches
As, free, she rolled over to face a woodland,
Smelled fungus, running water, and meadow,
Saw women in short tunics striding
With soldierly gait, but these were no soldiers.
They lifted her up and called her sister.
Iphigenia knew how to be grateful.
When it was said later she served at the temple
Of Artemis in the dusty heart of Tauris,
It was by those who had never seen her bounding
Like a hind from one rock to another.

Psyche

I do not dine on corruption
Any more than you, Dan C.,
Dine upon ecstacy;
It is rather the stripping
Of butterfly wings
That strings
Your bow and fletches arrows
Of arrogant rapture.
Capture
My heart, make your mother
See my iridescence
In my essence.
I am not spinning silk
When I search for sweetness,
Sweetness,
I search for you, small prince.
My life's work is to
Hold a candle to you.

JOY HOWARD

Beyond Casablanca

Journeying in high-born company
the pride of the desert
we come to an early oasis
not a scheduled stop   the riders
make to pass by
noses in air and haughty
cheeks averted
no betrayal
of the cause   no weakness
death
were preferable

Me   I rein in my camel
joyously   seeing dying as no
great shakes
careless of tomorrow's possible
transactions
today
is my business

We exchange one look   farewell
the caravan
the noble purpose of our journey
dust   I see
the promise in your golden eye
and know that travelling
to Samarkand
goes on wherever there's you and me
and water

Tetrahedron

I

Oh come   Pandora   surely you
can bring yourself to
open me
a crack
come now   aren't you a little
interested?
don't you feel   amidst
your understandable anxiety
a small sweet shiver   a desire
to know
what's in me?

I am just
a plain undecorated casket
insignificant   one among many
only if you choose me
shall I have earned
capital letters   you
might give me a name   I could
be known
down endless ages as
'Pandora's box"
imagine that

Together
we could be famous
are we to remain   merely
a faintly curious but hesitant
woman   and six square sides
of unvarnished wood?

You ask me what you're
in for?
I can't tell you   only say
on cool grey days I feel
the faint uneasy

Joy Howard

stirrings
of a high wind coming
from the west
a warmth from occasional sun
like the seeds
of huge tropical trees
a dampness   in the air
that could turn
into torrents
and a distant rumble
of thunder
that's all   and it may of course
be nothing.

If nothing   well then I'm still
a useful if rather ordinary
container
and yours   if you need me
if all   why
Pandora   we may
discover Atlantis or drown
in the venture

Come then   turn
the lock
fling your caution
to the four winds
I only ask   think
twice   before you
throw away the key

II

Ever since Eve   I've known
the dangers of curiosity
only they never taught me
how
to put out the burning
you're right   I am tormented
with thirst for your secrets

68

This key?   well I found
it by accident   some
sly guard must have left it
lying about on purpose
to tempt me
look how it gleams
dully in my shaded
palm   how it twirls
restless in my fingers

Here I stand   uncertain
with your smooth dark
wood
caressing my hand
your little lock inlaid
with pearl   inviting my touch

It should be so easy   why
do I feel as though
the fate of the world waited
on my decision   I am only
Pandora   daughter
of the dry mountains
and lover
of the sea

And you?   only a small
box   animal
vegetable and mineral
and not fearful
or only a little
of the fiercer elements

So you too want to try
for Atlantis?   and maybe
like me   you don't go
for package tours
and we may not get this chance
again   true enough
and the key

Joy Howard

shall go with us   I
will wear it with
my amulets   and it shall never
leave us

Be ready   yes
I am coming

III

So you think do you
both of you
that I
am yours
that I belong
in a lock
that I will be kept
as an amulet?

Beware!   I am not
for possessing
I am small   but
slippery
I shine   but I do not
lead the way

And while each of you
searches
for the Lost City
I may
quietly drop
through a crack among the rocks
between the roots of a tree
into the foam of the waves
under a coverlet of fine sand
gone
for good
leaving you to make
the best of your own ways
home

70

Whatever happens   do not
say
I never told you so

IV

Look to the sea
sun-flecked
unguessable
Atlantis
is mine

On Call

The phone rings and pulls me
like a netted fish   reluctant
struggling   to stay in the sea   and how
I needed to be asleep
this night
but   I fall
out of the net and into
the feathered softness of your voice
and turn into
one of those silly ducklings
who identifies
the first moving living thing it sees
as its   mother/guide/mentor
and will paddle around after her
all day

So before I can stop myself   I am
rolling in feathers again
and making little cheeping noises
of joy and contentment
when what I should be doing

Joy Howard

is giving you my
prepared speed
my platformed dignity

How like you
to home in on me this way
when my defences have been downed
in sleep   a difficult day
and a couple of gins

How like me
when I have sworn
on the heads of my past lovers
never to come near
your little finger   again
to let myself be twisted
like yarn from the fleece
around your spindle
I do protest   but its too late
already
the weaving has started
there is a pattern   familiar
emerging in the fabric
old jokes   like diamonds
form in the weft
in no time   it seems
we have our magic carpet
once more   at our feet

This time   please not
Xanadu

EMMA GREENGRASS

Diving

Not dragged
so much as dived in
Head first.
She said.

I said
I jumped
Not knowing if I
could swim.

It comes in waves, you know
I said. She said:
Let's hope we are not
drowning. I don't think so
but you never know.
As events turn out
I may, or may not be
Treading water.

I could have swallowed an ocean
there's enough salt in my mouth
tonight. No flares to bring me home.
I am up to my ears in it.
Keep going under.

Not dragged
So much as dived in
Head first,
She said.

And I?

Too busy diving
to agree.

Cider

I got drunk
for the first time
on cider.

Slurred my words
and staggered.
My, what a blur
of an evening.
It was wonderful.

The second time
I unceremoniously
(and with great
gusto) threw up
all down myself.

Several washes
on the 'Heavily Soiled'
programme could not remove
the stain from my coat.

After that
I avoided cider
for years.

It became
one of those drinks
you associate with
being 14, and drunk.

I didn't want
to be reminded.

Then one night
I don't know what shocked me more -

the tang of cider
stinging my mouth
again

or the first
taste of you -

salty and unexpected.

Green Windows

There was a pause
for thought
at the weekend.

I bought green paint
sandpaper, white spirit
and the wrong sort of tape
to stop myself painting
on the window panes
by mistake.

Painstaking work
scrapping *that* off the glass.
It took me the whole
following week
to remove.

I was there with my
butterknife
squinting directly
into the sun.

I gave myself such a
headache.

scrape…
        scrape…
                scrape…
But that night,
the night of the painting
I was close to ecstatic
stopping only to swig
my vodka and admire
my handiwork.

I learnt by trial and error
how not to paint
a window-frame.

To avoid that bumpy
dust-sprinkled-finish,
it's important to let
the dust settle, *before*
slapping on the paint.

Painting when drunk,
is not a good idea…

Oh - but it was worth it all
the following day
just for that first
breathtaking
splash of colour
as I opened the door.

It reminded me
I could do it on my own,
I didn't need you
to show me
how.

JENNY FACTOR

Amazing Grace

What I learned is life can be like that morning
on your bed's blue shammy when your kind mouth so
opened me to the street beneath your window,
we came out and shared our breakfast with the old
woman collecting

bottles on your corner, stood hand in hand to
watch girls' ebony knees fly gleaming through their
jumprope rainbows, so alive near you I cried
for the boy whose switchblade curved in a jeans' back
pocket. Or like that

windy day we walked to the duck pond where you
kneeled in mud to show Lev squirrel tracks crossing
shoe marks. After noon in the winter trees, we
saw the heron return in mating plummage;
Spring in ice, budding.

Then my poems milked you of tears. You lay like
sunlight on the wide sofa while I dared to
stroke your skin beneath the pillows Lev threw on
us, as he climbed over and I reached under,
laughing and laughing.

Gray days I come from my home's dismemberment
to your bedroom, stiff, trying not to listen,
not to be struck by your white shoulders. Then your
fingers raise my heart beneath them til I can't
tell what's skin, what's soul.

Rules of Engagement

A place behind her eyes I cannot go.
Green the day and red the sunlight there.
I hesitate. I speak. My words move slow

Reformulating tentative as prayer
What might reach to her eyes. She says, "I'll go
A little ways with you." We walk. I carry

In my pack an earthward tug. She knows –
Or spots – intensity, but There and There
She speaks in lightness, though her whispers open

Softly into mouse-steps of despair.
These gain me access to her hall, her room. And so
She on her bed, I in a chair

Begin in story; end in yes and no –
Our architecture built of character.
Her eyes in history and moonshadow,

Her eyes that dilate, earnestly aware
Onto a precipice, then shut. Read: no.
But tremble every limb, the truth is there

In "Stay!" and "Stay!" just as I turn to go.
What moves beneath her thin tracing paper
White skin? And should I trust her eyes' half-open

Door through word-dazed air? I do not go.
I hesitate. I speak. My words come slow.

Going Down the Mountain

Full of our ambition
We climbed the fireroad
On a hot day
Above the herd of live oak
Grazing Strawberry creek.

Looking down into those gnarled solutions
We talked of hopes big and small
Until we came to a slope
Flaming with California poppy.

There you made me stop
While you bent down to touch
The silky purse of the poppy
With your hand

And stuck your nose so deep
Into the flower
It must have reached
The Chinese tassel at the center
And grazed each pink-sheened surface.

Then you stood up smiling
As if you had found the only coin
Either of us would ever need.

The Art of Love

There it hung, my abstract canvas,
perpendicular divided blocks
of black and white, no bleeding line

intimated confusing grey into its divided form.
Impassive, it reduced
human representation to functional distinctions

imploding the consciousness of time
and space into neat, twine-tied parcels

which you unpicked.

Marriage

In our unspokeness lies
the acceptance which years
have proved

       our unspokeness lies.

PAM PARKER

Twenty

We are not to simplify
they tell us
how words attach to the world
but how complex
is it "Sixth and A"? Three
syllables
and there it is
the corner, laid out funny,
the buildings, with their bottom
fringe of grafitti, renewed
asphalt slick under rain
shiny with moving car lights
how my heart would rise
knowing she'd be there
as promised, hoping she'd feel
that bubble, expansive
and fragile. I called it love.
I think that was the right
word, and if not, it was close,
I was close, on Sixth and A
to heaven or something very like it
and twenty, I found it
simple.

ELANA DYKEWOMON

Passing for Not Unusual:
Conditions for Graduation at 48
(excerpt from a portmanteau)

I don't want to be cute about this. It's too easy to say in the academy
people talk to other people in the academy

too easy to say: I have the revolutionary vision   I am the pure
                                    cultural worker

I am as pleased as the next writer by my own cleverness
want a street named after me
was delighted that a dyke I met in the s.f. women's bath house said
after she read my first novel
she dropped out of college and went on the road

the language of fragmentation is definitely the end of millennium language
piece by piece
we know ourselves in shards

yet the impulse   my impulse   is to cohere   adhere
stick like velcro
gather the words like a sheep dog
herd us all
away from the cliff

use the word   anti hierarchically
in struggle with my own need

all that early women's movement poetry –   so much of it was garbage
wave after crashing wave of jane loves jane and daddy did me wrong
still
progressive movements
need poetry
and people hungry to change their lives
look for the words to say it

press their hands their foreheads against the cool letters

it's hot here   isn't it?

in this little box
where I try to define
the simple juncture
of the corner

Elana Dykewomon

A lesbian's prerogative

It's a lesbian's prerogative to run her hand down the seam
        across the seam of need
        and stick her finger in
        where the stitch is loose

a lesbian prerogative
        to pull at the thread, rip it apart
        demand the womyn
        start over

a lesbian prerogative to name herself:
        I am here before
        naming begins   before
        phyla and genera   I am
    the species who laughs
        looking at herself in the water
        who crows across the
        the river basin: beware
                my name is hot pepper and sea salt
                my name is spice
                I must be used
                with knowledge of effect
        I change the chemistry
                of the day I enter
                I am the hidden reactor
                I have a half-life of millennia

I can be forced   turned to stone
        underground   I can be hidden
        in storehouses   untapped
        my name can be erased from
        the pillars and tombs
                                still I come back

I am the lesbian lesbians are afraid of –
                the one who says
                you can't have it easy
                it doesn't work both ways there's

no polite company   no
diligence with which
you can coin a phrase
that will change the root
of men's culture
and make it safe

it's a lesbian prerogative
to prophecy
to rant and demand
a clear enemy defined
when she becomes a moving target
to expect her friends
to track the source
of what harms us

it's a lesbian's prerogative
never to apologize
to rip at the seams until
she's satisfied
and, once satisfied,
to doubt satisfaction
and start again.

desire, jews, casino

I
she dreams of dripping water
a flooded race track.
the bets are all
in a foreign language which
might be spanish might be hebrew   she isn't sure
she hasn't studied
when her grandfather was alive
they came out to the track
like a picnic, like a baseball outing
jews like to gamble a friend says
where you find casinos
there are jews
the week in tahoe didn't go well still
she picked up the tip to
always play machines
near the doors or food lines
the house likes noisy visible scores

tonight she has an urge   to get back in the car
and drive up there
the middle of the night   who cares now
there's a days food in the feeder for the cat
she could go anywhere
tired of desire being attached to womyn
you can attach desire
to four of a kind   to a royal flush
desire is like a leech it can fasten its mouth anywhere
it doesn't really need flesh or touch
the rough hull of a boat will do   any fast car anything shiny that moves

II
was that you?
complaining about desire?
complaining about desire and being a jew?
wanting a quick risk
a way to beat the odds
wagering what you get from the culture's hate:

'o you jews are all so smart'
against your own fear of loss –
quick – watch those cards
it can be gone in a flash
or is it guilt, jew, to have even a week's worth of extra cash
here
take it,   enmesh me endlessly in this drama about jews and money

about america and money   about jews and america and money
the big casinos on the western lake
knowing just how much we can afford to lose
balancing loss against win
fear of money and the true sins of money
with the fear of death
of growing old in debt
fear of the knock on your door   genetic
fear of not having a bribe ready
when they come for you

III
or was it lesbians and desire?
would you start across the valley, into the sierra at midnight
because you don't live with your lover anymore
because you have no lover and you're tired of lovers
and you wish your old lovers
still wanted to touch you
wish you still wanted to touch them
wish that desire wasn't such a leech
siphoning vitality from your veins

until what's left is a collection of games
you can't bear to play
facing anyone more intimate than the dealer
the dealer doesn't know you
but she knows your face
she can see in your face desire's ash
rolling for a seven, laying a stack on twenty two
gambling is something you can do with your hands

you know it.   tonight you resist the desire

to blow it shooting craps until four
but it doesn't change the way desire has you pacing
tracing your shadows in blood
you want
to take your desire
and attach it
once and for all to belief
on something that's safe
if not as bright as a slot machine,
if not as beautiful as her face,
then you demand
to desire yourself
want to believe you can own
your own reactions

you're still that naive

IV
o midnight eye
scowling across my dreams
I have a hard time losing money to machines
though I do it now and then
waiting for the perfect chance
and even if I say
there's nothing useful in romance
if it came gleaming through the night   if she smiled at me just right
I'd go

haven't I written this poem before?

it's so easy to repeat yourself in midlife
waiting for the trick the knack
the winning streak that
leads out of the casino

Tell me a story

"Let's say we have a mystery guest
she has turquoise skin—"
I lie in the shallow of your armpit
waiting for the story to begin but really
I want to tell you how I lived in a turquoise house once
the only turquoise house on the block
because my mother was in the hospital and my father
had it painted as a surprise,
how shocked, aggrieved my mother was
how I wanted to be like my father,
paint a whole house in colors no one else used
for fun, for the hell of it.
I want to ask now that you've met my father
and you can see how like him I modeled myself,
witting and unwilling,
do you still love me
for my simple lesbian ingenuity?
Do you love me as one-who-comes-from-a-family
as well as for this fierce orphan independence
I take? Quick, I want to say, tell me quickly –

We were all at dinner and the two of you were talking law
and I saw the way the boats moved up and down
on their moorings, the way the bay darkens as night
infuses the water
– your sex darkens sometimes that way
from a change in the atmosphere that appears
to come from underneath –
that's what I want to say: the surface can shine from
some ordinary or even horrible thing happening
and that happening, which we attribute to ourselves,
may not be ourselves at all,
but we walk around pleased with us, strut, almost,
convinced we're originals, while we mirror our families or place,
not even having the grace of precise observation.

I am quiet and looking at you
– your sex darkening from a change in atmosphere

that seems to come from underneath…
"Comfortable?" you ask me
and I shift my weight until my face is as close
to your scent as I can make it be
cinnamon and sweat,
some dry, rusty, calming smell and the smell
of coconut oil from your neck,
"Yes," I say, "comfortable.
Tell me a story."

JACKIE KAY

From Stranraer, South

Looking back, I can say, with my hand on my heart
that my mother got sick the day I said I was in love
with a girl who lived round the corner -
and never got better.

So Aileen McLeod left the day after my mother collapsed.
She caught the afternoon train from Stranraer, south.
My mother wouldn't open her mouth -
- and never got better.

Friends brought me news of Aileen, here, there,
and she herself sent me two letters.
The first said come now; the second don't bother; yet my mother
never did get better.

I don't know if it's me or if it's her, but I'm sure
a certain expression of satisfaction crosses her cheeks
when I give her a bed bath, as if she's taught me a lesson -
it will never get better.

I see myself in our hall mirror smiling my mother's smile,
complicit, apologetic, I know what you're up to.
No matter what I do I can't wipe that look from my face.
It will never get better.

I carry in holy water. I lift her head. Tilt her chin.
I dab round her smile with soft flannelette.
I bring the commode and stroke her hand. Fresh sheets.
It will never get better,

better than this, for what is a life for but to be a good daughter
and love your mother's weakness and moisten her lips
and listen to the sound of her dreams in waves
and see the stars outside flicker and waver, uncertain.

Maw Broon Sees a Therapist

Crivens! This is jist typical.
When it comes tae talking aboot me,
well, A' jist clam up. Canny think whit
tae say.

Weel, weel. A'm here because
A' canny hawnle life, ken whit A' mean,
because everything is awfy
and A'm no masell.

A' dinny ken who Maw Broon is anymare.
A' canny remember ma Christian name.
A' remember when A' wis a wean,
folks cried me something.

The idea o' me ever being a bairn
is impossible. A' feel A've aye worn
this same pinnie and this heid scarf
A've got on the noo.

How come you've no got anything tae say?
You've no opened yir mooth.
Whit's wrang. Am A' no daeing it right?
A' dinny ken hoo yir supposed tae dae therapy.

Jings. Aae A' jist talk on like this?
Michty. This is awfy awkward.
You've no said a dickie bird.
Tell you a dream? Crivens.

A've no had a dream since A' wis a wean.
An image? Whit kind of image?
What comes tae mind?
Whit represents whit?

Och. This therapy's making me crabbit.
A' thought this wuid mak me happy.
This is awfy. A' feel unweel.
How dae A' see masell?

Weel. Am fed up wey ma bun.
It is jist a big onion
at the back o' ma heid.
A' canny let ma hair doon.

A'm built like a bothy, hefty.
A'm constantly wabbit and crabbit.
Ma hale faimily taks me for grantit.
A'll aye be the wan tae dae it

whitever 'it' is. Here - A'm quite guid
at this therapy lark eh?
Here, Maw Broon could be a therapist.
Sit there like you are, glaikit,

a box o tissues and a clock,
a few wee emmms and aaas.
Jings, it's money for auld rope.
There that's whit A' feel like -

a tatty auld rope
nibiddy wuid want tae climb
a' twistit and tangled
an, jings, this is exciting

A' could break. A' could jist give in.

Jackie Kay

The Black Chair

Now I am inside the room
after all the dreaded waiting;
a woman is kinder, more gentle.

So you have me open my mouth;
I open it gladly for you.
Tiny mirrors, softly you tell

your assistant the language of ivory:
my vowels, my consonants, my country.
It is all unfathomable to me

but it sounds beautiful, rhythmical.
I could be crumbling, spotted with decay;
maybe need a filling, a cap, root canal.

My abscess is a mystery, a swollen book.
You tuck me up and put me to sleep.
My soft swollen gums are stroked, all red,

my tiny dark holes prodded
by one of your strange foreign instruments.
They lie at my side now gleaming

sharp as a family, smiling in a silver album.
I am laid back on your director's chair -
the pink glass of champagne at my side.

Every so often I rise for a moment
like a woman rising from a dream of the dead
like a woman standing up on a horse

to drink and swirl and spit and watch
my own frothy blood spin and disappear.
You say good, good, you're doing fine,

again, again, till your voice is a love song
and every cavity an excuse for meeting;
floss is the long length of string

that keeps us parted. My mouth is parted.
You are in it with your white gloved hands
I have not eaten garlic for weeks.

But you don't need to pull any teeth
alas, no molars to come out in your hands
no long roots, no spongey bits of gum.

We won't go that far. No. It's surface stuff,
really. Not nearly as deep as you or I could go.
You'll polish them. You'll give the odd amalgam.

You'll x-ray. You'll show me the photo.
I'll look at my own teeth on the white screen
They tell me nothing about myself.

My teeth, speechless.
Rootless pearls, anonymous white things.
I need you to tell me about myself.

Will the gaps widen with the years?
Do you know the day my grandmother died was hot, baking?
Can you tell I like sex from the back row?

I'd like it now, on this black chair that you move
up or down, bringing me back to life
telling me in a cheerful voice. I'm done.

JEWELLE GOMEZ

At Night

I want to hold you
in a motel room
with the sunshine stripe
of venetian blinds
across your back.
Or I want the dream of that.

My large breasts press down,
you drink my sweat,
I push inside
hoping for endless night,
mining for release.

Against the white sheet
you are young supple limbs
and dark thought.
I fear your newness,
my need to make you old.
All my words prelude
to this command of your body
locked in half secret by solid bands
of afternoon and evening
painted across the room.

Your hand is firm
in the rope of my hair.
The highway circles outside
and day blinks by.
You bend over me
and the shadow is not cool.
I want to press my mouth to your sighs
sucking in your insistent movement.
Or I want the dream of that.

ROSIE BAILEY

Now
(for my father)

I've forgotten the fear.
Now it's only sadness for our
Chronic mutual hatred.
It's what you missed that haunts me now,
The things I take for granted: credit cards;
Black-and-Decker short cuts;
Trouser-presses, car-phones, the M18;
The faceless undemanding reliable
Comforts of Forte. Fax.

No need now to check the windscreen-wipers
Before you take off for Leeds;
No need now to chat up the waiters or chambermaid
At the best hotels in town;
No need now for those lonely
Late-night trysts with the old Imperial. You'd still be
Up with the lark, of course - but now
You'd get much further ahead of the others
On the links, on the long road west.

I would give you this world,
If I could, old enemy, now.

Rosie Bailey

It's Good to Talk
(BT advertisement)

Just let me tell you this, you'd say.
I didn't listen. One eye on the clock
And halfway to the door, my mind
On half a dozen urgent things at once.

Yours was the chatty generation.
Dinner dance, coffee morning, luncheon club,
Ladies' night: you shone at all of them.

My silent brother, his silent sons and me -
We are perhaps great-uncle Johnny's heirs,
That secret sepia absentee
Who came and went and came and went
And never said a word.

Now I would like you to know
I wish I had listened more.
Just let me tell you this.

The Past

Is something you left in the top drawer
On the right hand side of the desk
That used to stand by the window
Overlooking the garden in the house
That has been for twenty years
A nursing home for the old and rich.
The room's familiar: green cord carpet,
Piano, landlady's ugly comfy chairs.
But you can't go in. It's as true
As the third step you take
When there are only two.

Sisters

Lily began life embarassingly soon.
Sensing this perhaps, she met events
With a sardonic frown. Complaint
And grumble were her tones. I caught
her taste for irony, practised
Raising my eyebrows in the Lily way.
I watched her lofty chic,
Snugging on Windsmoor, Jaeger, Worth.
I liked her gloomy jokes, her mild
Stationmaster husband. Her cakes.

Norah's eyes were snapping blue.
Unspecial middle child, she made her mark
On surfaces and corners. Comfy grime
Fled her terrible scour, like timid Will,
Eloping to his cabbages and beans.
Don't get me wrong, she'd say, before some
Demolition job. She wasn't cross with me.
No one liked to ask why her brief affairs
With the Church, with the Women's Institute
Ended so fast.

Both disapproved of good-time Gracie. Her goings on.
Flicks, lipstick, hairdoes, dances. Boys.
Much she cared. The ugly sisters could stay
At home. There's foxtrotting quickstepping
Major Chapman; dear doomed Bev's
Last slow waltz. I relished her racy
Unorthodox kindness. *Cheer up*, she'd say,
After some disappointment, *I'll let you read 'Secrets'*
(forbidden) and *'Flame'*. Or (under her bed)
No orchids for Miss Blandish.

Watersheds

Somewhere along the way
There must be a place
Where rain stops, and the road
Is all of a sudden dry. Or somewhere
A breath in the night where the radio's voice
Slips into dreams. The edges of things,
Where *now* becomes *then*.

You sense it sometimes when a leaf
Drops or an ambulance
Cries round the corner and you know
That for somebody - for all of us -
Things will be different. A change
Of the light. A glimpse
Of how it will be. In the middle
Of worry, haste, boredom, laughter,
The post goes. Letters. Photographs.
Dust.

7:30 A.M.

Here is the day again
Crisp as a starched shirt
Smelling as bright.

Look what the darkness
Puts it through: those ghosts.
Those midnight doubts.
The end-of-everything
At two a.m. And yet

Here are the cats wanting breakfast
As if nothing had happened.

Toothpaste, marmalade, tea:
Even at the end
This is how it will be.

NAOMI REPLANSKY

In the Woods

They walked in the world together
And came to the end of play.
Each of them clung to the other
And each pushed the other away.

That forest was not so scary,
And two should be warmer than one.
But each was so scared for the other
They shivered in spite of the sun.

And each so resembled the other,
Fear saw only its twin.
Neither could harbor the other,
Though skin touched answering skin.

Then they stood and swore at each other
To stop that trembling inside,
Till a chill came forth from their bodies
And the leaves that touched them died.

The birds flew off with the crumbs,
Thundercloud rolled overhead,
And at last they fled from each other,
In grief and relief they fled.

The Dangerous World

I watched you walk across the street,
Slightly stooped, not seeing me,
And smiled to see that mixture of
Clumsiness, grace, intensity.

Then suddenly I feared the cars,
The streets you cross, the days you pass.
You hold me as a glass holds water.
You can be shattered like a glass.

The Oasis

I thought I held a fruit cupped in my hand.
Its sweetness burst
And loosed its juice. After long travelling,
After so long a thirst,
      I asked myself: Is this a drought-born dream?
      It was no dream.

I thought I slipped into a hidden room
Out of harsh light.
In cushioned dark, among rich furnishings,
There I restored my sight.
      Such luxury could never be for me!
      It was for me.

I thought I touched a mind that fitted mine
As bodies fit,
Angle to curve; and my mind throbbed to feel
The pulsing of that wit.
      This comes too late, I said. It can't be true!
      But it was true.

I thought the desert ended, and I felt
The fountains leap.
Then gratitude could answer gratitude
Till sleep entwined with sleep.
      Despair once cried: No passion's left inside!
      It lied. It lied.

Naomi Replansky

When I Melt Down

When I melt down in your furnace
I want to take shape in your mold.
Blast me, cast me, change me,
Before the wind turns cold.

Look, from the red-hot center
I lift up my white-hot face.
My nose finds it bridge as always,
My eyes flow back into place.

Neither destroyed nor diamond
I walk from the core of your flame,
The rain does not hiss when it hits me,
And I answer to my old name.

JAN SELLERS

Pantoum for a January evening

A chill, damp winter evening, and the rain
turning to sleet, and gusting down the road;
brown leaves, old, windswept, drift along the lane.
I want you home, to laugh away my mood.

Turning to sleet, and gusting down the road,
ice, rain, obscure the windows where I wait.
I want you home, to laugh away my mood
as night draws on; it's bitter cold, and late.

Ice, rain, obscure the windows where I wait;
the firelight flickers, warming up the room
as night draws on. It's bitter cold, and late
for solitary travellers, trudging home.

The firelight flickers, warming up the room;
the sleet slacks off, and suddenly, you're there,
a solitary traveller, trudging home
in darkness, cold and chilled, with rain-soaked hair.

The sleet slacks off, and suddenly you're there;
I run to stir the fire to leaping flame.
In darkness, cold and chilled, with rain-soaked hair,
you laugh, call out; the evening's not the same -

I run to stir the fire to leaping flame
and draw you in, to warmth, and food, and light.
You laugh, call out, the evening's not the same -
I can shut out the cold, the sleet, the night

and draw you in, to warmth, and food, and light.
Brown leaves, old, windswept, drift along the lane;
I can shut out the cold, the sleet, the night,
the chill, damp winter evening, and the rain.

Jan Sellers

The wish of the daughters of Lot

We have known angels
who killed.
Our city was wiped out,
our mother dead
with all our kin, except
father, he who is all we have.

I would have stayed
with the angels if I could
or stayed in Zoar
with unenchanted men
and ordinary gods.

In this cave
father watches us
and we watch him
and hope his prayers
go unanswered

we love him
we are his
we hope he dies

Snails

As snails, we would spend summer days
out by the garden wall;
basking like cats, or basking sharks,
and not think much at all.
But, as the evening shadows grew
and warmth retreated fast,
we, like others of our kind
would think of love at last.

Warm and wet in the evening sun
my trail would link with yours
and as each felt the other's trail
each snail would turn, would pause,
would sample with a horn or two
the taste and scent, to find
the sweet perfume of slow desire
that each had left behind.

And we, with dedicated love,
but not in haste, would meet,
there by the rusty garden gate
or by the wooden seat;
and with our horns would touch, and stroke,
and smell, and feel, and taste,
as snails should do, who know desire
builds better, without haste.

There, in green shadows, we would lie,
your shell held close to mine;
twisting and turning, skin on skin
would slide, enfold, entwine.
Hidden amidst the waving grass
in dew, or summer dust,
there in the garden's evening light
we'd consummate our lust.

What need of hands, or legs, or tongues
when my whole foot can be

lips, hands and legs and tongue, in one
to hold you close to me?
Shell cleaves to shell, and foot to foot
and silver from us drips;
we roll and weave in the first moonlight
in a snail's apocalypse.

Home, Sweet Home

Because they said I could not build with stone
or brick or wood, I built my house with cake:
with ginger carved to look like sculpted bone
and biscuit slabs that took five hours to bake.

Angelica is beading for the door
and marzipan, the greeting on the wall,
and rock-hard icing for the pale green floor,
with skirting boards of chocolate in the hall.

In the dark woods, my trail of sugar flowers
shows children how to find their way to me.
They've wandered far - it takes them hours and hours;
I comfort them with sticky buns and tea.

I turn the boys into small garden gnomes;
and teach the girls to make their own Sweet Homes.

The messengers

Small faces, in the dark. A steady gaze
incurious and still, in lapping waves;
waiting, silent, staring up at the pier.
Their eyes meet mine; and send a sea-deep fear
washing through me, salty, sudden. The shifting haze

of night drifts, cold as death; these long harsh days
have driven the seals from their isolated ways,
from the rocks they haunt at sea, to meet me here:
small faces, in the dark.

Small dark skulls, wet, grey, childsize. I'd erase
this sight if I could, these silky heads which raise
their eyepits like some wordless messenger.
Night, and no light. My thoughts are chilled, child-clear,
remembering other faces, long-dead days;
small faces, in the dark.

U.A. FANTHORPE

Titania to Bottom
(for Alistair and Becky)

You had all the best lines. I
Was the butt, too immortal
To be taken seriously. I don't grudge you
That understated donkey dignity.
It belongs to your condition. Only,
Privately, you should know my passion
Wasn't the hallucination they imagined,
Meddling king and sniggering fairy.

You, Bottom, are what I love. That nose,
Supple, aware; that muzzle, planted out
With stiff, scratchable hairs; those ears,
Lofty as bulrushes, smelling of hay harvest,
Twitching to each subtle electric
Flutter of the brain! Oberon's loving
Was like eating myself–appropriate,
Tasteless, rather debilitating.

But holding you I held the whole
Perishable world, rainfall and nightjar,
Tides, excrement, dandelions, the first foot,
The last pint, high blood pressure, accident, prose.

The sad mechanical drone of enchantment
Finished my dream. I knew what was proper,
Reverted to fairyland's style.

                              But Bottom, Bottom,
How I shook to the shuffle of your mortal heart.

Counting Song

One man and his dog
Went to mow a meadow.

Not always the same dog,
But the man looks the same, disposable,
Scrapped. Hungerford Bridge his meadow.

This is the city we come to when we're young,
With the golden pavements. Where office-workers whisk
Like weir-water over zebras; where 15s and 77s
Snuffle down bus lanes, showy as heralds.

One woman and a baby

Probably borrowed, we say, not looking,
Moving on. We need to move on.
Our shoes are embarrassed. Our shoes are what she sees.

There's less of sky, now the great Lego thumbs
Angle their vacant heads into the gullspace,
But the saints watch us, Martin the beggars' friend,
Bride in her wedding-cake hat, and Paul,
Skywise and circumspect, sitting out centuries
Under his helmet, Thames washing past,
Refusing to run softly.

One gran and her bottle
Have given up on mowing.

These are waste people, grazing in litterbins,
Sleeping in cardboard, swaddled in broadsheets
And Waitrose plastic bags, who will not be recycled,
Must lie where they fall.

These are the heirs, the true Londoners,
Who work in this stern meadow. The others
Are on their way to somewhere else:
Statesmen and filmstars, remote, chauffeur-driven;

Volatile journalists, folding themselves in taxis,
As homegoers fold themselves into introspection
And the *Evening Standard*.

Written on Hungerford Bridge in letters of chalk:
Save Our Earth. Save Twyford Down.

Save Earth. Save Twyford Down. Save every one.

KATE FOLEY

Not For The Academy
(Berthe Morisot: Un Percher de blanchisseuse)

Not a good drying day.
Factory chimneys on the plain's edge
send up skittish plumes loaded with smuts
that may veer.

Smalls and sheets
translucent with soap and soda
hang limp as discarded skins
on the gap toothed comb of a fence.

From here you can't smell
the pug-nosed wrinkle of sewage,
but you guess their feet
are planted muck deep.

Thick armed women,
bodies branching to the taut snap
of a line, bending like a community
of trees from a more elegant picture.
Faces smeared with a sweat of paint
break through, blossoming pink suns.

Their lives are laid out in squares
framed from an upstairs window.
Not the golden vee
of a measured landscape,
but the faint yellow disappearance
of stained crotch and armpit
getting ready to fly in flags of plain white.

Kate Foley

Portrait of a Whistling Woman

"A whistling woman
a crowing hen
does neither good
to god nor men…"

Snapping like a turtle
Mother St Birchman said it,
her frill gophered round her face
like tiny holders for Woodbines.

Bare knees wincing
on the woodblock floor
I knelt before pink plaster Jesus,
pinned out decorous as a lace fan.

All I'd done was whistle
but she came down like a fast bowler,
as if she guessed where whistling
might go.

Why should he have all the tunes,
that small, holy light in the tabernacle,
or the pink Christ with neat flat loincloth?

I met him before I knew
he'd created black and white,
x and y, no shades in between.

Didn't Artemis ever take a whistle
from her breeches and sit in the shade
slim fingers poised, each hole
a well of silence, till breath
muscle and reed sculpted the sound?

Now I am painting a self-portrait,
layering on shadow, researching
the exact shade of yellowish pink
and lavender, trying not to flinch

116

at badger bristle of lip and chin,
but my lips purse soundlessly
and my head cocks, listening
for a woman who whistles that tune
hidden in the brown throat of summer.

The Great Blue Heron
(for Adrienne Rich)

is not a symbol,
but a bird, with blue feet
that can't freeze,
its complex central-heating
system described by zoologists.

You reach past your own words
for the full fishy delicate sense
of its otherness and are not afraid
of it trampling with great
calligraphic strides over the mudflats
and trapped clouds of meaning.

It matters - as matter
is the blue slipstream of its plumage,
green on the red of your retina
if you close your eyes -
to be patient in the autism
of otherness, flowers breaking
from the grass like fireworks,
your own life a Verey light
sprung from the ocean's hairline,
signalling presence;

a warm bloodknot
creaturely in the dark
where your whole heart
strives on your lips.

Red Shift

Glass so red it holds
the whole falling sun
is only copper shavings
in a clear matrix.

but when I put my fingers
to my crotch and they came away
scarlet for the first time,
when my mother showed me
the stained yellow yolks
soft from a hen's secret sac,
when my hands dipped in birth blood
and a baby flooded crimson
with its first cry, red
had entered my hopes,
fat and tasteable as a pomegranite.

And now that red is an absence,
though its' metal taste and rich smell
once ripened in every room,
now that it has blackened
like old varnish,
I need to find common nouns
on the other side of colour
that will stand up
plain and bleached
to be my furniture and luggage.

Don't Be Quiet

Someone in a white coat
told me plainly today,
don't be quiet, don't go on
about beauty, that little
seed in your breast casts
a long shadow.

So my heart has got a bruise
like a finger-print. I look
at other women, bagged up
carefully around their own
cracked hearts, shoulders
protective as flying buttressess;
at their eyes, flinching
as if death is too important
for them to claim;

and love grates on silence,
solid as dry beach
under my keel of bone.

Kate Foley

Heavy Water

If in your gentleness
you sometimes forget
that love is not the only truth
we know, then I'll remind you,

you taught me first
our histories, like heavy water
in our veins, can't be denied.
To live after them

as if an empty page
or a clear stretch of stream
were open, is not in nature.
We have to bear them written

in our blood. I see you
watch me read, and in your deep
kindness long to wipe the page.
You won't. You are looking

for something longer than love
and braver than kindness.

Here's the House, Where's the Steeple?

How do I know your hands
tell me the truth? Because
mine cannot lie.

Stripped of carefulness
in the strong disinfectant of truth
they're naked, no longer ready

for easy, familiar gestures,
for wooing or soothing
when they should fall silent in my lap.

When your hand crept cold,
sweaty, trembling, into mine,
no words were said,

but mine, trembling back,
confirmed the invitation.
Your hands are limber,

nimble, good at making
gothic steeples,
while mine make roman arches.

But used to the last resource
of touch, each neuron fired,
fingers speaking in tongues,

our hands lie, resting quietly
after the work of love,
in the earned interlace of silence.

BIOGRAPHICAL NOTES

ROSIE BAILEY:
Born in 1932 in Northumberland and educated at Whitley Bay
Grammar School, Girton College, Cambridge and St. Anne's
College, Oxford. Taught Spanish at Cheltenham Ladies College,
and later became lecturer and then Principal Lecturer in charge of
Humanities undergraduate programmes at the University of the
West of England. Belongs to Gloucestershire poetry workshop,
walks the dog, paints, prints, and has published *Course Work*
(Culverhay Press). Combined with UAF in *Double Act* (Penguin
audiocassette), 1997), in which she do the police in different
voices.

JUDITH BARRINGTON:
is an Anglo-American poet and memoirist. She is the author of
two collections of poetry and editor of *An Intimate Wilderness:
Lesbian Writers on Sexuality*. Her most recent book is *Writing the
Memoir: From Truth to Art* and her memoir, *Lifesaving*, will
appear in spring 2000. She is the founder and co-director of Flight
of the Mind, Writing Workshops for Women, and President of
Soapstone, a women writers' retreat. She lives in Porrtland,
Oregon with her partner of twenty years, Ruth Gundle.

ELANA DYKEWOMON:
has been a U.S.-based lesbian cultural worker and radical activist
for thirty years. *Beyond The Pale*, her Jewish lesbian historical
novel, won both the Lambda Literary and Gay Lesbian
Publishers' awards for lesbian fiction in 1998. Other works
include *Riverfinger Women* (one of the first dyke novels of the
'70s), *They Will Know Me By My Teeth* (stories and poetry), and
Nothing Will Be As Sweet As The Taste (poetry, Onlywomen
Press). She was editor of the international lesbian feminist literary
journal, *Sinister Wisdom*, from 1984-1995. Currently teaching
English at San Francisco State University, living happily with her
partner among friends, she tries to make trouble whenever she can.

JENNY FACTOR:
graduated from Harvard and Radcliffe Colleges summa cum
laude in Anthropology in 1991. She has worked as an

archaeologist and as a preschool teacher, and is currently enrolled in the MFA program in poetry at Bennington College. She lives with her son in New York, USA.

U. A. FANTHORPE:
Born in 1929 in Kent, educated at S. Catherine's, Bramley, and St. Anne's College, Oxford. Was Head of English at Cheltenham Ladies College (where she met RVB), then made a break for it and worked at various off-beat temporary jobs in Bristol. Finally settled as clerk/receptionist at a small neuro-pyshiatric hospital, where poetry hit her. Six collections published by Peterloo Poets, two selections and an audio cassette published by Penguin. Looks after the cats, distributes the type, but is too lazy for the dog.

KATE FOLEY:
was born and brought up in NW London. She first knew she wanted to be a poet aged 11 at her convent school. In 1994, very much later, after a varied career as nurse, midwife, teacher, archaeological scientist and conservator, all of which fed into her poetry, Onlywomen Press published her first collection, *Soft Engineering*. Her second collection, *A Year Without Apricots*, is forthcoming (Blackwater Press).

JEWELLE GOMEZ:
is the author of the award winning novel, *The Gilda Stories*, which she adapted for the stage and was performed by Urban Bush Women in 13 U.S. cities in 1996. She is also the author of a collection of essays, *Forty Three Septembers*, a collection of short stories, *Don't Explain*, and three books of poetry. The most recent is titled *Oral Tradition* (Firebrand Books).

EMMA GREENGRASS:
Born 1967. Grew up in Clacton-on-Sea 'with fond memories of white stilettos and jumble sales'. She made her escape from Essex in 1986 to study Eng. Lit. at Hull University until 1989. Moved to London after her degree 'to get a high powered job in publishing'. Took secretarial work with the publishing arm of a development agency and stayed there for five years, before deciding that neither the 'high powered job' nor 'publishing' was what she wanted. Currently a PA by day for a well known UK charity, and a

performance poet by night, Emma has made her home in the East End with her bicycle, and without a cat.

CAROLINE GRIFFIN:
Born and brought up in the Midlands. Having moved to South London in 1973 and gone on living, working and sharing in bringing up our (beautiful) daughter here, means I call this my home. I still live communally (just) in a women's house with an increasingly flourishing garden and still teach in a local boys' Comprehensive school. The pursuit of poetry-in living, writing and reading is my necessary expression. Music, good food, friendship, loving and being loved also help to balance and celebrate this precarious journey on which we are embarked.

J.P. HOLLERITH:
was born in Canada and has lived in England for 18 years. Her previous work has been published in England by Onlywomen Press, Virago, and Poetry Now. Under the name, Caro Clarke, she has published short fiction and a novel in the USA. She works in publishing and lives in London with her partner and the necessary cat. Her life-sized labyris, pride of her collection, has recently been joined by a fencing épée, which one day she hopes to wield with distinction.

JOY HOWARD:
is getting on a bit now, signing up for the Looking Forward to Retirement course and hoping there'll be time for lots more gardening. She has lived in West Yorkshire for the last 10 years, and would be out there campaigning for the virtues of entrenched domesticity, but is too busy enjoying them to get out of the house much. She acknowledges the fault, and feels obliged to place some of the blame on her dearly loved partner, Barbara, who makes it all not only possible but also desirable. Poems published – all prior to this unlooked for but happy state of affairs – can mainly be found in 3 anthologies of the late eighties: *Beautiful Barbarians* (Onlywomen Press, 1986), *Dancing The Tightrope* (the Women's Press, 1987), and *Naming The Waves* (Virago, 1988). that feels like long ago – it's good to be sharing some poems again.

MARIA JASTRZEBSKA:
was born in Warsaw, Poland in 1953 and came to Britain as a
small child. She is the author of *Postcards From Poland and other
correspondences* (Working Press, 1994) with artist Jola Scicinska.
She was one of the editors of *Forum Polek* - The Polish Women's
Forum, a bi-lingual anthology. Her work appears in various other
anthologies, most recently *As Girls Could Boast* (ed. Christina
Dunhill, Oscars Press, 1994) and *Knowing Me: Women Speak
About Myalgic Encephalomyelitis and Chronic Fatigue Syndrome*
(ed. Caeia March, The Women's Press, 1997). She lives in
Brighton.

JACKIE KAY:
was born and brought up in Scotland. She has published three
collections of poetry for adults – *The Adoption Papers* (winner of a
Forward Prize, a Saltire Award and a Scottish Arts Council Book
Award), *Other Lovers* (which won the Somerset Maugham
Award) and *Off Colour* – all published by Bloodaxe. She has also
written three collections of poetry for children – *Two's Company*
(which won The Signal Award), *Three Has Gone* and *The Frog
Who Dreamed She Was An Opera Singer* (Bloomsbury). Her
novel, *Trumpet* (Picador, 1998), recently won the Guardian
Fiction Prize.

JANE MILLER:
An American poet, has recently published *Wherever You Lay
Your Head* (Copper Canyon Press). Among earlier collections are
Memory At These Speeds: New and Selected Poems; *The Greater
Leisures*, a National Poetry Series Selection; and *August Zero*,
winner of the Western States Book Award. She has also written
Working Time: Essays on Poetry, Culture and Travel, in the
University of Michigan's Poets on Poetry Series.

RUTH O'CALLAGHAN:
has published in *The London Magazine*, *The Honest Ulsterman*,
Quartos and *Acumen* in addition to being included in anthologies
and winning a minor prize in a poetry competition. She is also
interested in playwriting and has had her work read at London
venues and performed at the Oval Theatre.

PAM PARKER:

Her work has appeared in *The American Voice, Conditions, The Kenyon Review, Penthouse Forum, Semiotext (e) USA, Western Humanities Review, The Persistent Desire* (Joan Nestle, ed. Alyson Publications, 1992), and *Doing It For Daddy* (Pat Califia, ed. Alyson Publications, 1994). From 1986 - 1989, she served as an editor for *Conditions* magazine. A resident of Manhattan, she works on Wall Street as a computer programmer.

MINNIE BRUCE PRATT:

her second book of poetry, *Crime Against Nature*, was chosen as the 1989 Lamont Poetry Selection by the Academy of American Poets, was nominated for a Pulitzer Prize, and received the American Library Association's Gay and Lesbian Book Award for Literature. She co-authored *Yours in Struggle: Three Feminist Perspectives on Anti-Semitism and Racism*, with Elly Bulkin and Barbara Smith. Her other books include *We Say We Love Each Other, Rebellion:Essays 1980 - 1991*, and *S/HE*, stories about gender boundary crossing. Her most recent book is *Walking Back Up Depot Street*, a collection of narrative poems about growing up in, and leaving, the segregated South, appearing in The Pitt Poetry Series, Spring 1999. She lives in Jersey City, New Jersey.

NAOMI REPLANSKY:

was born in the Bronx, New York, in 1918. She has been writing poetry since she was 10, but writes slowly. Her first book, *Ring Song*, was published by Scribner in 1952 and was a finalist for the National Book Award in poetry. In 1988, a chapbook appeared. In 1994, *The Dangerous World: New and Selected Poems, 1934-1994* was published by Another Chicago Press. She has worked in offices and factories, and as a medical editor, computer programmer, translator, and teacher. She now lives and writes in New York.

ALEIDA RODRÍGUEZ:

is a Cuban-born poet whose work has been published in many journals, textbooks, and anthologies since 1973, including *In Short: A Collection of Brief Creative Nonfiction* (W.W. Norton, 1996), *The Spoon River Poetry Review* (Editors' Prize winner, 1996), *The Kenyon Review, Prairie Schooner, Ploughshares,*

ZYZZYVA, and *Sleeping With One Eye Open* (University of Georgia Press, 1999). Recipient of numerous awards, including a National Endowment for the Arts fellowship, her work was also nominated for a Pushcart Prize. *Garden of Exile*, (Sarabande Books, 1999) was selected by Marilyn Hacker to win the Kathryn A. Morton Prize. She lives in Los Angeles, where she works as an editor and translator.

MAUREEN SEATON:
is the author of four books of poetry, most recently, *Furious Cooking* (University of Iowa Press, '96), winner of the Iowa Prize for Poetry and a Lambda Literary Award; and a collaboration with poet Denise Duhamel, *Exquisite Politics* (Tia Chucha Press, Chicago, '97). She has been the recipient of an Illinois Arts Council grant, an NEA fellowship, and other awards. Her poems have appeared in *Ploughshares, Paris Review, The Atlantic, New Republic, The Pushcart Prize XX and XXII*, and *The Best American Poetry 1997*.

JAN SELLERS:
teaches study skills at The University of Kent at Canterbury. She divides her time between Canterbury (work and research) and London (partner, cat and research, not always in that order). Her poetry has appeared in a number of journals and in anthologies published by Virago, The Women's Press, Oscars Press, Centerprise and The Community Projects Foundation. Most recently, her work appeared in *Love Shook My Senses*, edited by Gillian Spraggs (Women's Press, 1998).

PAT WINSLOW:
worked for twelve years as an actor in England, Ireland and Scotland and left the theatre in 1987 to take up writing. Her short fiction appears in *Herzone* (Crocus), *No Limits* (Crocus), *Queer Words 1, 2 and 3, Bridport Winners Anthology 1993*. Her collections of poetry include *The Fact of an Eye* (Amazing Colossal), *Harvest* (Jackson's Arm). Her poems are included in *Beyond Paradise* (Crocus), *Five Women Poets* (Crocus). She has received the BBC's Alfred Bradley Award and a short fiction bursary from North West Arts.

ACKNOWLEDGEMENTS & PERMISSIONS

Rosie Bailey:
"Now", "It's Good to Talk", "The Past", "Sisters", "Watersheds" and "7.30 A.M.". all appear in *Course Book*, Culverhay Press, 1997.

Judith Barrington:
"The Dyke With No Name Thinks About Landscape" was the 1996 winner of the Dulwich Festival Poetry Prize and was first published in *The American Voice*. "Why Young Girls Like To Ride Bareback" and "Four Reasons for Destroying a Spider's Web" appeared in *The Kenyon Review*. "Body Language" was first published in *Fireweed*. "Horses and the Human Soul" won the 1998 Clackamas Review Poetry Prize.

U.A. Fanthorpe:
"Titania to Bottom" appears in *Neck-Verse*, Peterloo Poets, 1992.
"Counting Song" appears in *Safe as Houses*, Peterloo Poets, 1995.

Kate Foley:
"The Great Blue Heron" and "Not For The Academy" appeared in *Ambit*. "Don't Be Quiet" appeared in *Blade, 1998*. "Red Shift", "Here's the House, Where's the Steeple" are in the prizewinners edition of *Second Light*. "The Great Blue Heron", "Not for the Academy", "Red Shift", "Heavy Water", "Here's the House, Where's the Steeple" appear in Ms Foley's collection, *A Year Without Apricots*, Blackwater Press. Leicester, 1999.

Marilyn Hacker:
"Languedocienne" appears in *Love Poems By Women*, Faber & Faber, London and with "Going Back To The River" among *Selected Poems* by Marilyn Hacker, 1994, Norton, New York and London; "Scars on Paper" was first published in the UK in *P/N Review*.

Jane Miller:
"The Flying Fish and Lily of May" appears in *Wherever You Lay Your Head* by Jane Miller, Copper Canyon Press, USA.

Minnie Bruce Pratt:
"The White Star" from *Walking Back Up Depot Street*, by Minnie Bruce Pratt, © 1999. Reprinted by permission of the University of Pittsburgh Press.

Maureen Seaton:
"When I Was Straight" first appeared in *Green Mountains Review*, Fall/Winter 1995-96, Vol. VIII. No.2, Johnson, Vermont.

Jan Sellers:
"Pantoum For a January Evening" appeared in *Orbis* magazine, 1989; "The Messengers" appeared in *Orbis*, 1990; "The Wish of the Daughters of Lot" appeared in *The Rialto* magazine, 1993; "Snails" appeared in *The Rialto* magazine, 1992; "Home, Sweet Home" appeared in *The Rialto* magazine, 1994.